A Guide to
Owning and
Caring for a Parrot

Tips for Training, Taming, Breeding
and Housing these Beautiful Birds

British Library Cataloguing-in-Publication Data
A catalogue record for this book is available from
the British Library

Aviculture

'Aviculture' is the practice of keeping and breeding birds, as well as the culture that forms around it, and there are various reasons why people get involved in Aviculture. Some people breed birds to preserve a specific species, usually due to habitat destruction, and some people breed birds (especially parrots) as companions, and yet others do this to make a profit. Aviculture encourages conservation, provides education about avian species, provides companion birds for the public, and includes research on avian behaviour. It is thus a highly important and enjoyable past time. There are avicultural societies throughout the world, but generally in Europe, Australia and the United States, where people tend to be more prosperous, having more leisure time to invest. The first avicultural society in Australia was The Avicultural Society of South Australia, founded in 1928. It is now promoted with the name Bird Keeping in Australia. The two major national avicultural societies in the United States are the American Federation of Aviculture and the Avicultural Society of America, founded in 1927. In the UK, the Avicultural Society was formed in 1894 and the Foreign Bird League in 1932. The Budgerigar Society was formed in 1925.

Some of the most popular domestically kept birds are finches and canaries. 'Finches' are actually a broader category, encompassing canaries, and make fantastic domestic birds, capable of living long and healthy lives if given the requisite care. Most species are very easy to breed, and usefully do not grow too large (unlike their larger compatriot the budgerigar), and so do not need a massive living space. 'Canary' (associated with the *Serinus canaria*), is a song bird is native to the Canary Islands, Madeira, and the Azores – and has long been kept as a cage bird in Europe, beginning in the 1470s. It now enjoys an international following, and the terms *canariculture* and *canaricultura* have been used in French, Spanish and Italian respectively, to describe the keeping and breeding of canaries. It is only gradually however (a testament to its growing popularity) that English breeders are beginning to use such terms. Canaries are now the most popular form of finch kept in Britain and are often found still fulfilling their historic role of protecting underground miners. Canaries like budgies, are seed eaters, which need to dehusk the seed before feeding on the kernel. However, unlike budgerigars, canaries are perchers. The average life span of a canary is five years, although they have been known to live twice as long.

Parakeets or 'Budgies' (a type of parrot) are another incredibly popular breed of domestic bird, and are originally from Australia, first brought to Europe in the 1840s. Whilst they are naturally green with yellow heads and black bars on the wings in the wild, domesticated budgies come in a massive variety of colours. They have the toes and beak typical of parrot like birds, as in nature they are climbers; budgies are hardy seed eaters and their strong beak is utilised for dehusking seeds as well as a climbing aid. When kept indoors however, it is important to supplement their diet of seeds with fresh fruit and vegetables, which would be found in the wild. Budgies are social birds, so it is most important to make sure they have company, preferably of their own kind. They do enjoy human companionship though, and may be persuaded, if gently stroked on the chest feathers to perch on one's finger. If not kept in an aviary, they need a daily period of free flight, but great care must be taken not to let them escape.

Last, but most definitely not least, perhaps the most popular breed of domestic bird, is the 'companion parrot' – a general term used for *any* parrot kept as a pet that interacts with its human counterpart. Generally, most species of parrot can make good companions. Common domestic parrots include large birds such as Amazons, African Greys, Cockatoos, Eclectus, Hawk-headed Parrots and Macaws; mid-sized birds such as Caiques, Conures, Quakers, Pionus, Poicephalus, Rose-Ringed parakeets and Rosellas, and many of the smaller types including Budgies, Cockatiels, Parakeets, lovebirds, Parrotlets and Lineolated Parakeets. The *Convention on International Trade in Endangered Species of Wild Fauna and Flora* (also known as CITES) has made the trapping and trade of all wild parrots illegal, because taking parrots from the wild has endangered or reduced some of the rarer or more valuable species. However, many parrot species are still common; and some abundant parrot species may still be legally killed as crop pests in their native countries. Endangered parrot species are better suited to conservation breeding programs than as companions.

Parrots can be very rewarding pets to the right owners, due to their intelligence and desire to interact with people. Many parrots are very affectionate, even cuddly with trusted people, and require a lot of attention from their owners. Some species have a tendency to bond to one or two people, and dislike strangers, unless they are regularly and consistently handled by different people. Properly socialized parrots can be friendly, outgoing and confident companions. Most pet parrots take readily to trick training as well, which can help deflect their energy and correct many behavioural problems. Some owners successfully use well behaved parrots as therapy animals. In fact, many have even trained their parrots to wear parrot harnesses (most easily accomplished with young birds) so that they can be taken to enjoy themselves outdoors in a relatively safe manner without the risk of flying away. Parrots are prey animals and even the tamest pet may fly off if spooked. Given the right care and attention, keeping birds is usually problem free. It is hoped that the reader enjoys this book.

Contents

INTRODUCTION

THE large family of Parrot-like birds which are to be found wild over a very large area of the world are in all probability the oldest type of caged bird. Records of Parrot species are to be found in the old writings of the ancient Egyptians, Chinese and the Incas of South America. Parrot-like birds have a special attraction to both old and young alike, undoubtedly because of their beautiful colourings, amusing antics and wonderful powers of imitating the human voice. In this handbook I have endeavoured to explain simply and concisely how Parrot-like birds should be managed to keep them in perfect health and feather, and the treatment they need to make them gentle, playful and good talkers. Although there are many different breeds of Parrot-like birds ranging from the gigantic Macaws to the minute Pigmy Parrots they all require a similar sympathetic treatment. I feel sure that for anyone looking for a pet that is unusual and amusing, a Parrot is ideal, and it is hoped that this Handbook will be helpful in the matter of selecting the right kind of Parrot.

HISTORY

IT has become quite clear after studying the history of the early civilizations in the warmer parts of the globe, that Parrot-like birds were kept in captivity both as household pets and in decorated aviary structures. When the first members of the Parrot species actually came to this country it is difficult to ascertain, but undoubtedly odd specimens were brought over by the early Traders from the near East. It is known that Alexander the Great brought tame Parrots from India to Rome where they became great favourites with the nobles of that time. The Romans housed their Parrots in cages made of ivory and precious metals and in most elaborate aviaries. Until the early part of this present century Parrots were mostly associated with sea-faring men and elderly ladies, although a few were kept by Aviculturists, but now their cult is widespread and embraces people in all walks of life. The advent of the long distance sailing ships brought seamen into contact with countries where Parrots were amongst the wild birds and were kept as pets by the natives of those lands. Brightly coloured, strange-looking birds that could imitate the human voice must have appeared very fascinating to those adventurous seamen and it is little wonder that numerous specimens of the various kinds were brought back to this country as gifts for their families. Some of the earliest specimens of birds from foreign countries to be housed at the Zoological Gardens, London, were birds of the Parrot-like species. At the present time the Zoo has a wonderful and varied collection of Parrots, Macaws, Cockatoos, Parrakeets, etc., and the Parrot house is always a centre of attraction for visitors of all ages.

BAN ON IMPORTATIONS

Up to 1931 when a ban on the importation into this country of all Parrot-like birds was imposed, vast numbers of Parrots of all species came into this country often under very crowded conditions and the mortality was often high. The fact that Parrots were so easy to obtain did little to encourage Aviculturists to attempt to breed them in this country. However, the application of the Parrot ban altered this outlook and quite a lot of Parrots, Parrakeets, etc., hitherto not bred in this country were reared by keen breeders. Because of the difficulty of breeding Parrot-like birds, and the fact that they could only be imported under special Government licence, made their value rise sharply and good talking birds or rare specimens could cost up to £100 each. In 1952 the Parrot ban was removed and once again Parrot-like birds have become more plentiful and consequently more reasonable in price. The ban was again imposed in the early part of 1953 and Parrot-like birds can only be imported under licence which should be applied for from the Ministry of Health, London. However, during the clear period, the stocks of Parrot-like birds in this country were replenished both as breeding birds and as pets. Air travel has made the importation of all kinds of birds so much more simple, and journeys which at one time took weeks can now be completed in a matter of hours. This quick method of travel allows birds to arrive in this country with little or no inconvenience and in a much better condition, consequently they are easier to acclimatize. The care and treatment of newly imported specimens are, as will be seen in Chapter 5, of utmost importance and actually control the length of the bird's life. Certain species of Parrot-like birds can live to a great age under favourable conditions and there are records showing they have survived over 100 years in captivity.

HABITAT

Parrots do not occur as wild birds (escaped specimens

excepted) on the Continent of Europe proper and their distribution lies mainly within the tropical and sub-tropical areas of the world. There are many groups of related birds all having the distinct articulated upper mandible and paired toes which together form the extensive family of Parrot-like birds. In the next Chapter each of these groups has been dealt with separately and a description given of the more popular varieties. It will be realized that in a small handbook like this, it is not possible to give a fully detailed account of all the many forms. Should the reader require further and complete descriptive information it can be obtained from the many excellent specialized bird books of individual countries. Practically all members of the Parrot-like groups can be taught to talk, but their proficiency varies with the different varieties and also with individual specimens. Some of the species such as the African Greys and the Amazons have tremendous powers of reproduction of the human voice and other sounds, whilst further kinds do not talk so fluently, but become exceedingly tame and friendly and can be taught to do various tricks.

COLOUR VARIETIES

Many of the Parrakeets and Love Birds breed quite freely in captivity and with some of the species, colour varieties have been raised and perpetuated. The principal new coloured breeds are the Lutino Ring-necks (yellow birds with red eyes), Yellow Redrumps and Blue Love Birds, all of which are most attractive forms. Other species of Parrots and Cockatoos have been bred occasionally, and in another Chapter the breeding of Parrot-like birds in this country will be dealt with in a practical manner.

VARIETIES

THE large family of Parrot-like birds can be divided into a number of different groups and representatives of all of them are kept here in Great Britain either as single pets or in collectors' aviaries. First come the typical Parrots, then the Macaws, Cockatoos, Conures, Love Birds, Pigmy Parrots, Parrakeets, Lorikeets and Lories. In the following paragraphs a description is given of the popular and most interesting members of each group commencing with the typical Parrots.

THE AFRICAN GREY PARROTS (*Psittacus erithacus*).
(Fig. 1)

There can be little doubt that these Parrots are the most sought after and most popular of all the vast number of Parrots. They are invariably of gentle nature, easy to handle, require a simple diet, have a long life and a capacity for imitating the human voice with great accuracy. The Grey Parrots are about 13 ins. in length with a dark-coloured, stout hooked bill and bare patches of white skin surrounding the eyes; their size varies somewhat, with the females generally a little smaller. The body colour is a shaded dove grey with a short vivid red tail and under covets. These and other African Parrots require special care when first imported, but once they have become acclimatized they are, if properly managed, practically trouble-free. Correct feeding plays an important part in keeping all birds in perfect health and in good hard plumage. A sound staple seed mixture should consist of about 50 per cent large canary seed (Spanish canary type) and the remainder made up

Fig. I. AFRICAN GREY PARROT

with equal parts of mixed sunflower seeds, safflower seeds, hemp, dari and a few whole oats and ground nuts. The actual percentages of the ingredients can be varied a little to suit the tastes of individual birds, but it is important that canary seed is always present in a good proportion. Chapter 4 deals fully with the feeding of all Parrot-like birds when they first arrive in this country and also when they have become acclimatized. As a general rule African Greys are most friendly and gentle birds and are quite safe with children and animals. Although they have powerful beaks which can crack nuts with ease they will only attempt to bite if frightened, teased or ill-treated in any way. Birds which have spiteful habits have invariably been badly trained and roughly treated when first caught, but with kindness they can usually be cured. Greys have been known to form strong attachments to dogs, cats, monkeys and other birds and a great many stories are told as to their various exploits. Once the confidence of the birds has been gained, the owners can do practically anything with them and with care and patience they can be taught to perform most amusing tricks.

TIMNEH GREY PARROTS (*Psittacus Timneh*)

These attractive Parrots are very close relatives to the birds described in para. 6, but are only imported occasionally because they are not so frequently taken by the native trappers. They are about 12 ins. in length which is slightly smaller than the common Greys and they are much darker in body colour throughout, with the tail and under covets being a dull reddish chocolate shade. Owners of Timneh Parrots all speak of their intelligence, gentleness and great powers of imitation. The general treatment, housing and feeding are the same as with the ordinary African Grey Parrots.

BROWN-HEADED PARROTS (*Poicephalus fuscicapillus*)

Another attractive type of African Parrot which has more variation in plumage than the Grey Parrots are the Brown-headed Parrots which are similar in size to that of the common Greys. Their head and neck feathers are silvery grey with rich brown centres and their foreheads a rosy red. The wing areas are a greenish brown shade and the butts of the wings and thighs are a red shade similar to that carried on the foreheads. Individual birds have been known to become very proficient talkers, but generally they are more reluctant to imitate than the Greys. However, what they lack in verbosity they make up for in tameness and brighter colouring of plumage.

SENEGAL PARROTS (*Poicephalus senegalus*) (Fig. 2)

Next to the Greys the charming friendly little Senegal Parrots are the most widely kept of all the many African Parrots. They are quite small birds between 9 ins. and 9½ ins. in length with dark grey heads and necks with lighter shading on the cheek patches. The upper part of the chest is green and the lower, in contrast, a bright orange yellow

Fig. 2. SENEGAL PARROT.

making a pleasing combination. Some birds show an extra amount of yellow in their plumage and it is thought that with a little careful breeding in captivity all yellow ones could be produced. Senegals are one of the easiest Parrots to train to perform tricks and are exceedingly gentle with their owners. Their powers to imitate seem to be somewhat limited although their enunciation is very clear and distinct. As with all kinds of Parrot-like birds, individuals of outstanding talking ability are met with occasionally. On account of their comparatively small size they are frequently kept in pairs in a normal-sized parrot cage. Senegals are equally gentle with their own species as they are with human beings. The antics of a pair of Senegals either in a cage or breeding aviary can be a constant source of delight and amusement to their owners. They are extremely hardy birds and once acclimatized will live a great many years without the least trouble in their health.

MYER'S PARROTS (*Poicephalus meyeri*)
These interesting Parrots are only imported into this

country in spasmodic consignments and generally their distribution is inclined to be somewhat localised. If the opportunity to purchase should ever arise it should be taken, either for a household pet or to add to a collection of Parrot-like birds. They are only small birds being round about 9 ins. in length and their primary colouring is brown, green and yellow. With care they quickly become very tame and some are quite talkative to their owners, but rather shy with strangers.

OTHER MEMBERS OF THE POICEPHALUS SPECIES

The following African Parrots are sometimes met with in this country, but the numbers imported are usually limited. BROWN-NECKED PARROTS (*P. rotustus*) head and neck grey-shaded with brown, body and rump green, wings dark green with thighs and wing butts vermillion red, overall length 13 ins., male and female similar in size. CONGO RED-HEADED PARROTS (*P. guilielmi*) top of head scarlet orange, body neck and wings green, thighs and wing butts same colour as head, overall length 11 ins. Near relatives to these Parrots are the *P. subryanus* which are a little larger in size and carry more red in their plumage. RED-BELLIED PARROTS (*P. rufiventris*) head, neck, wings and back rich brown, centre of chest and under colouring of wings bright red, lower chest and thighs green and yellow, rump green, overall length about 9 ins. with some variation between the sexes. RUPPELL'S PARROTS (*P. ruppelhii*) head, neck and back smokey brown, wing butts and thighs deep yellow, rump greenish blue ; charming little Parrots of about 8½ ins. overall length. From the island of Madagascar come the giant GREAT VASA PARROTS (*Coracopsis Vasa*), these are very large Parrots of about 20 ins. in length and are of a smokey brownish-black colouring throughout with the skin surrounding their eyes bare and whitish in colour. Their beaks are mostly horn coloured. The Great Vasas and their near relatives, the LESSER VASAS (*C. nigra*), are mostly kept in aviary collections as they have not really attractive features to recommend them as household pets, although individual birds have been known as great pals.

THE SOUTH AMERICAN SPECIES

From South America comes a very wide range of Parrot-like birds and for the sake of simplicity in this Handbook they have been divided into the following groups : Macaws, Amazon Parrots, various South American Parrots, Caiques, Conures (macaw-like Parrakeets), Parrakeets and Parrotlets. Of this enormous number of Parrot-like birds the Amazon Parrots are by far the most popular and the majority of these Parrots make excellent talkers.

THE MACAWS

Macaws are a group of large, long-tail, bright-coloured birds with tremendously powerful beaks which can crack nuts such as Brazils with the greatest of ease. Their size ranges from about 13 ins. to 39 ins. according to their species. Individually-kept birds are as a general rule not very noisy, but when pairs or more than one species are kept together in a confined space they can create a very great deal of sound. Owing to their very powerful beaks they must always be housed with this thought in mind and also they must at all times be handled carefully. They are not as a rule very fluent talkers, but can be tamed to an amazing degree considering their size and powerful beaks.

HYACINTHINE MACAWS (*Aodorhyncus hyacinthinus*)

When in full plumage these Macaws are said to be the most handsome of all these wonderfully coloured birds ; they are large in size being about 39 ins. in overall length of which about 24 ins. are taken up by their long tapering tails. Except for their dark beaks and yellow-tinted naked skin around their eyes they are a most beautiful deep hyacinth blue colouring throughout. Owners of these birds have always remarked how gentle and good natured they are, providing they are reasonably young when taken as pets into a household.

RED AND BLUE MACAWS (*Ara chloropters*)

These and those in the next two paragraphs are probably the best known and the most widely kept of all the Macaws. The Red and Blue Macaws are two or three inches smaller

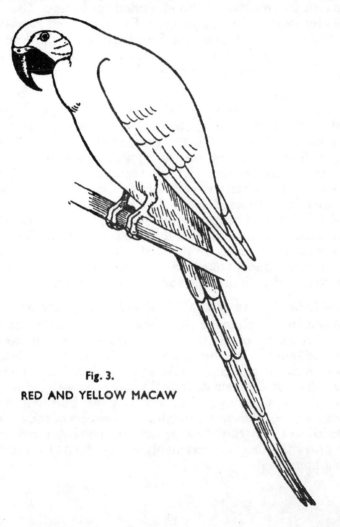

Fig. 3.

RED AND YELLOW MACAW

than the Hyacinthines and their plumage is attractively coloured in red, blue and green. Their bright colours and amusing antics always make them particularly attractive to children with whom they are invariably most gentle.

RED AND YELLOW MACAWS (*Ara Macao*) (Fig. 3)

Similar in size and general behaviour to the Red and Blue Macaws, their plumage colouring is red, yellow and blue in a most striking arrangement and their beaks are light horn coloured on top and dark underneath with the bare cheek patches pinkish white.

BLUE AND YELLOW MACAWS (*Ara ararauna*)

These are smaller birds than the two previously mentioned Macaws, being generally about 30 ins. to 32 ins. in overall length ; their main colours are blue on the upper parts of their bodies and yellow on the underparts and the under surfaces of both wings and tail. Their beaks are dark coloured and very powerful. However, they can be quickly tamed if taken in hand when young, but their vocal powers of imitation are of a somewhat limited range although their natural voice is very powerful indeed.

MILITARY MACAWS (*Ara militaris*)

These are sometimes called the Giant Green Macaws because of the large amount of green colouring in their plumage ; their beaks are dark, their heads red and blue, their flight feathers blue, rump and underparts of tail blue, upper parts of tail red and the remainder of the body colouring, various shades of green. They are said to be very easy to handle and make delightful pets.

OTHER MEMBERS OF THE MACAW SPECIES

The following Macaws are occasionally imported into this country and young birds of the different kinds mostly make good household pets. HAHNS' MACAWS (*Diopsittaca*

Hahni) these are quite small for Macaws being only about 13 ins. long, their main colour is green on back and dull red on wing covets and underparts with a bluish tint on their foreheads. ILLIGERS MACAWS (*Ara Maracana*) smallish birds, about 16 ins. to 18 ins. in length mainly green in colour with red patches on underparts. These birds have been bred in captivity several times and the young reared successfully. SPIX'S MACAWS (*Cyanopsitta Spixii*) pleasing birds of a silvery, greyish-blue colouring which is set off to advantage by the dark naked skin patches surrounding their eyes.

THE AMAZON PARROTS

Next to the African Grey Parrots in popularity come the Amazon Parrots in their many different kinds. The Amazon Parrots have the largest number of different species in any one group. The prevailing colour of the Amazon is green ornamented in different ways with many shades of red, blue and yellow. The powers of imitation possessed by some of the species of the Amazons is remarkable and as a general rule all the species are hardy and easy to train. Some Amazons live to a great age and their abilities as linguists rival those of the best African Greys.

BLUE-FRONTED AMAZONS (*Amazons aestive*) (Fig. 4)

These Parrots are about 15 ins. in overall length which is the average size of the Amazon group. Like all of their species their main colour is green with blue on their foreheads (which gives them their name) running into yellow on top of their heads, cheeks, throat and upper chest, wings edged with red. Blue-fronts are imported in greater numbers than most of the Amazons and have much to recommend them as pets. They are hardy, gentle with their owners, quick to learn and speak with a clear tone.

YELLOW-FRONTED AMAZONS (*Amazons ochrocephalà*)

These are very similar in size and in general behaviour to the Blue-fronted which they press closely for popularity.

Fig. 4. BLUE-FRONTED AMAZON

They are very like the Blue-fronted in their colour except that the blue forehead is replaced by bright, clear yellow which fades into a greenish shade at the back of head; edges of wings are red.

GOLDEN-NAPED AMAZONS (*Amazons auro-pallista*)

These are very delightful birds of an inch or so less in length than the two aforementioned species. As their name indicates, their outstanding feature is the deep yellow colouring on their necks ; their foreheads are yellow to yellowish green and the edges of their wings and secondary flight feathers are red.

YELLOW-SHOULDERED AMAZONS (*Amazona ochroptera*)

These are not quite so frequently seen in this country as the Golden-naped although their owners always speak most highly of their good nature and their capacity for learning. Their main colour is green edged with black, with top of head, face and throat yellow fading into white on the forehead. The chest and lower neck bluish with the wing butts yellow.

FESTIVE AMAZONS (*Amazona festiva*)

These birds are a little more colourful than most of their group and make very attractive pets. They are of average size and their main colour is bright green with a dull band of red on forehead and red on rump, with blue on cheeks, throat and streaks over the eyes.

SOME OTHER MEMBERS OF THE AMAZON GROUP

There are some forty other species of the Amazons, specimens of which are seen from time to time and it is not thought necessary to give the names and details of all of these birds. However, the following may be met with a little more frequently. LEVAILLANTS AMAZONS (*Amazona oratix*) head and neck yellowish-white with deeper colour on cheeks and light-coloured beaks, wing butts yellow and red, lower covets also red and the remainder of the plumage green. GUILDINGS AMAZON (*Amazona guilddingii*) one of the largest of the group being about 17 ins. in overall length. Head white ; neck light green ; back, underparts and wing covets rich light brown with wings of green, orange and blue. MEALY AMAZON (*Amazona farinosa*) head yellow ; neck and upper parts mealy ; edge of wings red, remainder of colouring green. ACTIVE AMAZON (*Amazona agilis*) these are one of the smallest members of the group being only about 10 ins. in overall length. Main colouring green with bluish tinting on top of head and red primary feathers.

VARIOUS OTHER SOUTH AMERICAN PARROTS

In addition to the large and interesting group of Amazon Parrots, a number of other Parrot species come from South America. The majority of these are quite brightly coloured

and will learn to talk in varying degrees of fluency : they
will all become quite tame if taken in hand when they are
young birds.

VIOLET PARROTS (*Pionus fuscus*)

These Parrots are delightful little birds of just over 10 ins.
in length ; their tail, under tail covets and flights are violet ;
head dull, deep blue ; back brown becoming pinkish at the
edges of the feathers ; chest greyish-purple. Violet Parrots
make very nice quiet attractively-coloured pets and quickly
become exceedingly tame and friendly. Their vocabulary·
is not usually extensive and the voice is small, but nevertheless clear. They are very friendly birds and similar in
practically all respects to the Senegal Parrots.

RED-VENTED PARROTS (*Pionus menstruus*)

These are near relatives of the Violet Parrots which they
resemble very closely in their general habits and behaviour.
They are blue on head, neck and upper parts of breast ;
back and underparts greenish bronze ; beak horn-coloured
and ear patches black ; the under tail covets vivid red
splashed with green and blue. There are several other
members of the Pionus group, but they are only seen on rare
occasions in this country.

HAWK-HEADED PARROTS (*Deroptyus accipitrinus*)

These are quite striking-looking Parrots of about 14 ins.
in total length. They are brown striped with buff on the
head which gives them their strange hawk-like appearance.
Their chest colour is red, edged with blue and the nape and
back of head feathers are blue tipped with red, with the
remainder of the body green in colour. Owners of these
birds say they become reasonably tame and take very kindly
to captivity and will, with perseverance, imitate a few words.

GREEN-THIGHED CAIQUE (*Pionites leucogaster*)

These are smallish birds of about 9 ins. to 10 ins. in overall length with rather shrill voices for ordinary household pets, but nevertheless they can be taught to talk and become very tame and playful. Their main colouring is green with head and neck orange and cheeks tinted yellow; chest patch whitish. Although not very strikingly coloured, these birds can be seen to advantage in an aviary in preference to a cage.

YELLOW-THIGHED CAIQUE (*Pionites xanthomera*)

As above, only with yellow colouring on their thighs: they are similar in size, habits and behaviour to the Green-thighed. BLACK-HEADED CAIQUE (*P. melanocephala*) only occasionally imported. Head black ; cheeks and collar deep yellow ; back, neck and wings green ; thighs, flanks and tail covets orange.

PARROTS OF THE MALAY STATES AREA

From the Malay Archipelago come several most interesting and beautifully coloured Parrots, foremost of which is the Eclectus group. In their wild state the Eclectus live partly on ripe sweet fruits, but they will thrive well on a mainly all-seed diet if they are initiated gradually to this method of feeding; they will, of course, need some fruit. They do not seem to have very great powers of mimicry and are rarely kept solely as pets although they will become exceedingly tame and most friendly with their owners.

GRAND ECLECTUS (*Lorius roratus*)

These are fine birds with the males being about 17 ins. in overall length and the females usually slightly less. The unusual thing about the birds of this group is that their feathers have a hair-like appearance in contrast with the smooth feathering of the majority of the Parrots. Also the main colours of the males are green and red whereas those of the females are red and blue, making the matter of sexing quite simple. The males are green with deep blue flights, under covets and large patches on their sides vivid red, the beak is red, tipped with yellow, which sets off their colouring to advantage. The females are crimson red on head, back, wings, rump and tail ; nape of neck purple and chest purplish blue and the beak black. These birds do make most decorative house birds and are not at all noisy, but as mimicry is not their strong point they are seldom seen as pets. Other Eclectus Parrots include the RED-SIDED ECLECTUS (*L. Pectoralis*), CARDINAL ECLECTUS (*L. cardinalis*), and WESTERMAN'S ECLECTUS (*L. Westermanni*).

RACKET-TAIL PARROTS (*Prioniturus platurus*)

These are smallish Parrots of about 13 ins. overall length, which includes their somewhat strange tail feathering. Their main colouring is green ; nape and mantle areas pink and lavender and the covets lilac. Their two central tail feathers are shaft-like with webbing at the ends only, giving them the appearance of two minute rackets, hence their name. These unusual birds are seldom imported, and being rather costly are found usually in the aviaries of large collectors. Two other unusual Parrots from the same area are the GREAT BILLED PARROTS (*Tanygnathus megalorhyuckos*), brightly coloured with very large powerful red beaks, and PEQUETS PARROTS (*Psittrichas pecquetii*), large birds with bare black faces and black elongated beaks.

SHINING PARROTS (*Pyrrhulopsis splendens*)

These are very beautiful birds of about 18 ins. overall length and come from the Fiji Islands area. Their head, neck and underparts are resplendent in shining crimson red ; nape of neck bright blue with the back and rump green. They live mainly on a seed diet, but they must always have a regular supply of fresh fruit and green food to keep them healthy and in full plumage.

HANGING PARROTS

These are quaint little Parrots of between 5½ ins. and 6 ins. in length which spend a great deal of their time hanging upside down from their perches. They feed on fresh fruit and a soft food mixture. There are several members of the group the foremost being the BLUE-CROWNED HANGING PARROTS (*Coryllis galgulus*), their main colour is bright green with a patch of blue on the crown and a yellow patch on back and lower rump, with a red spot under the lower part of the beak. These little birds are not talkers and are invariably kept because of their unusual habits.

COCKATOOS

These are a rather wide group of fairly large birds which are inclined to be noisy when excited. As a general rule Cockatoos are great talkers, and even if they do not say as many different words and sentences as the Greys and Amazons they make up for it by repetition. Cockatoos are always attractive birds because of their colouring and their beautifully tinted crests which they can raise or lower at will. Taken collectively Cockatoos are most friendly both to other birds and to human beings and are very amenable to being trained. They have a reputation for living to a great age and are very easy to feed and manage and seem equally at home in cages, on stands, or in aviaries.

GREAT SULPHUR-CRESTED COCKATOOS (*Kakatoe galerita*)

There are several kinds of the Sulphur-crested Cockatoos or Lemon-crested as they are also called, which are more or less commonly known, ranging from the Great which are about 20 ins. in overall length to the Dwarf which are just over 12 ins. in length. The general colour of these birds is white and the crest and ear covets are sulphur yellow with the beak black. As a general rule these large Cockatoos are kept chained by a leg on parrot stands which allows the birds a certain amount of extra freedom of wing movement. The chains are very light, strong metal, and do not cause the birds any inconvenience. Like most of their kind they are very fond of bathing. Owners, of these and several of the larger Cockatoos mentioned in the following paragraphs, say how gentle these big birds are. They seldom attempt to bite even when provoked. The Author knows of a Great Sulphur-crested who has as his constant companion a little Blue Budgerigar and will not settle down for the night until he has seen his little friend's cage placed close by his side. It is quite common for large Parrot-like birds to form strong attachments with quite small birds of a different group.

GREAT WHITE-CRESTED COCKATOOS (*Kakatoe alba*)

These are another species of fine large birds of about 18 ins. overall length and are entirely white throughout including the crest, with the exception of the naked skin surrounding the eyes which is blue tinted, and a black beak. The dark colouring of eye and beak area gives these birds a far more attractive appearance than it would if they were all plain white. Many of these birds make excellent talkers especially so if taken into training when young.

GREAT BLACK COCKATOOS (*Proboscigar aterrimus*)

These are the largest of all the Cockatoos being about 30 ins. in overall length. They have very large crests, particularly when raised, and their beaks are long and extremely powerful. Their colouring is a uniform black with a greenish gloss throughout, although generally speaking the colour appears to be on the greyish side owing to a natural white dust which comes from the base of the feathers and skin. All Parrot-like birds have this peculiarity, but it only really shows up on birds with very dark or black plumage. The naked cheek areas are wrinkled and of a deep reddish colouring. They are only striking because of their size and unusual sombre colouring, but are not generally counted as being ideal pet birds. A few black Cockatoos have been known to talk reasonably well with a clear rather bell-like tone. There are several other black Cockatoos of which the BANKSIAN COCKATOOS (*Calyptorhynchus Banksii*) are the best known and probably the most widely kept. They are more colourful and not so large as the Great. Their colouring is mainly glossy greenish black with a wide crimson band on tail with the cheeks and neck speckled with yellow, this yellow and red colouring on the black gives these Cockatoos a rather pleasing appearance.

LEADBEATERS COCKATOOS (*Kakatoe Leadbeateri*)
(Fig. 5)

These are medium-sized birds of about 16 ins. overall length and their colouring is quite pleasing and gay. Their

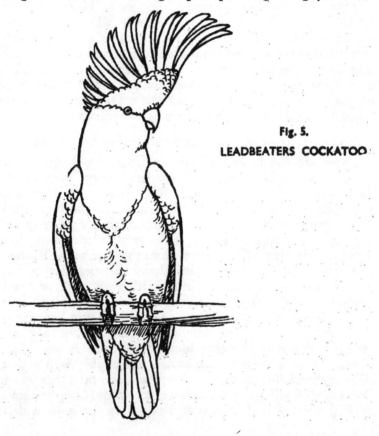

Fig. 5.
LEADBEATERS COCKATOO

crest colour consists of bands of white, red, yellow and red which is seen to special advantage when fully erected. The rest of their colouring is white heavily suffused with a fine soft rosy red giving a lovely effect. Leadbeaters make very delightful household pets as they are very amenable to training, quickly learning to talk and mimic and are not generally given to using their own natural rather shrill voices too freely. One particular bird, Bill by name, was great friends with a Cocker Spaniel dog, and the two of them spent many happy hours playing together in the garden. On winter evenings Bill delighted in sitting with the dog by the fire playing with his ears—much to the Spaniel's enjoyment !

ROSEATE (OR ROSY-BREASTED) COCKATOOS
(*Kakatoe roseicapilla*)

These are the most popular and certainly the most widely kept of all Cockatoos both in their homeland, Australia, where they are called Galahs, and numerous other countries. They are one of the smaller kind of Cockatoos being about 14 ins. in length and most delightfully coloured in white, rose pink and grey. The crest which is white suffused with pink mostly lies flat to the head, being raised when the birds are pleased, startled or annoyed. The neck, chest and underparts are a lovely shade of rose red and the upper parts, wings and tail are of a soft grey, the tail being slightly darker than the rest of the body. Roseate Cockatoos are friendly little birds and quickly become tame and very attached to their owners. Their talking ability is somewhat limited, but the voice is clear and sharp. Although their beaks are small for Cockatoos they can nevertheless do quite a lot of damage if given the opportunity, many of them seem to have a great liking for digging out the putty from window frames. However, taken all round, Roseates are excellent birds for domestic pets, and another point in their favour is, given the right surroundings they will breed in aviaries in this country.

OTHER COCKATOOS

There are a number of other varieties of Cockatoo which are occasionally to be found as pets or in collectors' aviaries, but the aforementioned ones are most frequently seen. One rather unusual group are the SLENDER-BILLED COCKATOOS (*Licmetes tenuirostris*) which have very long, narrow beaks from which they get their name. They are mainly white in colour with head, neck and breast feathers flecked at their base with bright red. Another type which are striking are the BLUE-EYED COCKATOOS (*Kakatoe opthalmica*), white-coloured birds with long drooping crests and naked patches of blue skin surrounding each eye.

CONURES

From South America come quite a large group of Parrakeets which are somewhat like Macaws in shape and ranging from about 7 ins. to 17 ins. in length. Conures mostly make good pets as they quickly become tame and friendly, but at times rather spoil themselves by their shrill noisy voices. Once acclimatized they are extremely hardy and will thrive well on canary seed, sunflower seed, a little rape seed and some fresh fruit.

ST. THOMAS CONURES (*Eupsittula pertinax*)

These are neat little birds of about 10 ins. in length and are one of the favourite Conures. The crown of the head is bluish-green with forehead, cheek, chin and middle of under parts orange, the remaining areas green. These Conures are equally at home as single pets as they are in pairs, although the antics of a pair are certainly most amusing to watch. Single birds will become very friendly and with patience can even be taught to say a few words.

CACTUS CONURES (*Aratinga cactorum*)

These are very similar in size and temperament to the St. Thomas Conures. The top parts of the body are green with the crown a dull slate ; cheeks, throat and upper breast brown with the lower breast orange.

QUAKER CONURES (*Myiopsitta monacha*)

These are very hardy birds and will breed fairly freely in this country. Pairs have reproduced quite well at liberty in the grounds of Whipsnade Zoo and it is quite a pleasing sight to see these Parrakeets flying and calling on the wing in natural surroundings. There is an unusual feature with these Conures, they actually build a nest of sticks in which to lay their eggs whereas the usual practice of Parrot-like birds is to nest in holes in trees or very occasionally in holes in banks on the ground. Quakers are about 12 ins. in overall length with the main colouring a fairly deep green ; cheeks, throat and chest grey with a scale-like appearance ; yellowish green on underparts and flanks. They make very nice pets and they can be taught to do tricks and also to say a few words.

GOLDEN (OR SUN) CONURES (*Eupsittula solstitialis*)
(Fig. 6)

These are really lovely birds of about the same size as the Quakers whom they resemble closely in general behaviour. They are mainly golden yellow in colour with wings and tail green and blue. The yellow colouring deepens with age and fully adult birds of several moults are a beautiful shade of golden orange. Golden Conures are most desirable birds both as single pets or as pairs in breeding aviaries. There are many other varieties of Conures that are seen in this country from time to time and some of them breed quite well if given the right conditions.

LOVEBIRDS (*Agapornis*) (Fig. 7)

True Lovebirds are small, short-tailed Parrots and are quite distinct from Budgerigars* (*Melopsittaucus undulatus*)

* These popular and delightful little Parrakeets are dealt with very fully in a separate Foyles Handbook *Budgerigars* by the Author. Price 4s.

Fig. 6. GOLDEN CONURE

which are often wrongly called " Lovebirds " .Lovebirds
vary in size from 5 ins. to 6 ins. according to species and the
majority of them breed quite well in this country and several
types have produced mutations of Lutino (Red-eyed
Yellow) and Blue. Taken generally, Lovebirds although
small Parrots, do not mimic or talk and only one or two odd
cases of talkers have been recorded. Although this is the
case it does not mean to say that more Lovebirds could be
taught to talk if they were persevered with when. young.
They will become extremely tame and friendly and breed
quite well both in cages and aviaries. The most popular of
the group seems to be the BLACK-CHEEKED LOVEBIRDS (*A.
nigrigenis*) which are dark green above and light green
below ; cheeks black ; top of head red-brown, with bib a
beautiful deep pink ; beak red. NYASA LOVEBIRDS (*A.
kilianoe*) are also quite popular with breeders and look very
smart with their green bodies, red-orange forehead, cheeks
and throat. PEACH-FACED LOVEBIRDS (*A. roseicollis*) are a
little larger in size than the Black-cheeks and make most

Fig. 7. MASKED LOVEBIRD AND PEACH-FACED LOVEBIRD

desirable birds for the breeding aviary. Their main
colouring is deep bright green with upper tail covets bright
blue and face and crown a lovely shade of peach pink.
There has been some cross-breeding between the above-
mentioned species, and also with some of the other kinds,
but breeders are now trying, and quite rightly so, to keep
the individual species pure.

AUSTRALIAN PARRAKEETS

From Australia and the surrounding islands in that area
comes a vast array of beautifully-coloured Parrakeets, quite
a number of which will breed in this country and many can
be taught to say a few words. As the list of species is so
very long to deal with they cannot all be fully described in
this Handbook. A few types have been selected to show
some of the beauties of these Parrakeets.

ROSELLA PARRAKEETS (*Platycercus splendidus*)

These are very handsome, popular and free-breeding birds with a lovely blend of colours and are about 14 ins. in length. Head, neck and chest rich scarlet which is set off by white cheek patches ; back black and yellow ; rump and tail covets yellowish green. The majority of Rosellas (there are several nearly related species) are hardy and docile birds and make tame and colourful pets.

RED-RUMPED PARRAKEETS (*Platycercus hæmatonotus*)
(Fig. 8)

These are probably the most widely kept of all the smaller Australian Parrakeets and they certainly have many

Fig. 8.

RED-RUMP PARRAKEET

good points to recommend them both as pets and breeding birds. They are about 12 ins. in length and are mostly gentle with other birds and their natural call is soft and musical. Head and face greenish-blue ; breast yellowish-green fading to yellow on the underparts ; back bluish-green and rump bright clear deep red. Red-rumps are excellent birds for any new Parrakeet breeder to start with as they are so easy and simple to manage. There is a Yellow mutation of the Red-rumps which although not quite so brightly coloured as the Normals are most interesting to breed. They are hardy little Parrakeets and will thrive well on a similar diet to Budgerigars to which a little sunflower and hemp seed has been added.

MANY-COLOURED PARRAKEETS *(Platycercus multicolor)*

These birds are similar in size and general temperament to the Red-rumps with whom they will hybridise. Head and cheeks greenish blue : forehead, shoulders and under-tail covets yellow ; nape red ; thighs and under-parts orange. These are extremely pretty birds and make a wonderful sight when flying in an outdoor aviary.

COCKATIELS *(Leptolophus hollandicus)* (Fig. 9)

These charming birds are sometimes called Cockatoo Parrakeets as on their heads they carry a permanently erected crest. Although more sombre in colouring than is general with Australian Parrakeets, Cockatiels have a quiet attraction of their own. They are hardy, friendly, free-breeding, have a musical voice and will speak a few words quite clearly. Their general colouring is dove-grey ; face, throat and cheeks yellowish ; ear-covets orange red and crest grey with yellow base. Single birds will get very tame and can be allowed the freedom of the house and some are so good they can even be allowed the freedom of the garden ! Cockatiels have been known to breed quite freely and happily in the same aviary as Budgerigars and small

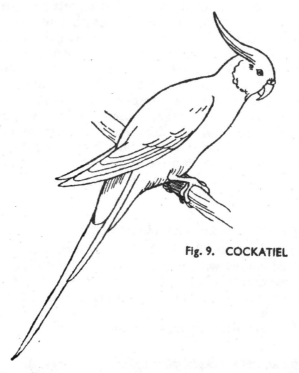

Fig. 9.   COCKATIEL

Foreign Finches and have not attempted to harm their small companions in any way. It is quite an amusing sight to see a cheeky little Budgerigar bossing a much larger Cockatiel about.

RING-NECKED PARRAKEETS (Fig. 10)

These are an interesting group of fairly large Parrakeets consisting of about a dozen different species of which the best known is the common Ring-neck. A great number of these birds have been brought to this country both by Service and Civilian personnel serving in the Indian area. They are probably the most common of all the " Polly Parrots " ! All the species can be taught to talk and the

Fig. 10.

RING-NECK PARRAKEET

extent of their vocabulary is governed by the particular
talents of individual birds and their trainers. The two
most commonly kept are the common Ring-necked Parrakeets (*Psittacula marillensis*) ; these are about 16 ins. in total
length including their long narrow tails. Their main
colouring is bright green with neck ornamented with a collar
of rose-red which is bluish at the top edge; moustache

Fig. II. SWAINSON'S LORIKEET

and eye streak are black, and beak red. BLOSSOM-HEADED
PARRAKEETS (*Psittacula cyanocephala*) : these are slightly smaller
than the common Ring-necked and are a little more sedate
in their demeanour. They are charming birds of very
gentle habits and are quite easy to train to talk. The head
is coloured red in front which gradually fades to a lovely
plum-bloom shade to the nape, below this is a black collar
broadest at front ; red patch on wings ; green on back and
greenish-yellow underparts.

LORIES AND LORIKEETS (Fig. II)

These are a group of beautifully highly-coloured birds
varying in length from 8 ins. to 12 ins. and differing from
the other species of Parrakeets in their feeding. These

lovely birds feed on a diet of nectar and soft fruits both of which are abundant in the countries where they live. Lories and Lorikeets are not ideal birds for household pets because of their feeding, although numerous specimens become very tame and will even say a few words. In aviaries, however, they display their gorgeous colours to the fullest advantage and make a wonderful sight when flying. Below, two examples are described to give the readers an idea of the glorious colouring of these birds. SWAINSON'S LORIKEETS (*Trichoglossus Swainsonii*), these birds are about 12 ins. in overall length with tail taking up just over a third of the total length. Head and throat blue ; breast yellow and red ; underparts red with dark blue patch in the centre ; back, wings and tail mainly green with some yellow. Swainsons have been bred in this country both in indoor and outdoor aviaries and seem to make very good and attentive parents. RED LORIES (*Eos bornea*) : these birds are slightly larger than the Swainson's which they resemble in many ways. They are practically all red in colour with wings marked with black and blue and the tail a dull golden red shade.

When You Buy a Parrot

Parrots and their kin are in their best condition in warm weather, since they are tropical or semi-tropical birds. Always purchase a parrot in the warm months. There is then little danger of the bird being chilled during transportation. Carry the bird in a tight draft-proof box, preferably a thick-walled wooden one, without bars. When you arrive home, transfer the bird at once to its permanent cage, which should be, for parrots, preferably one with three wooden sides and a barred side. Cover this cage lightly with a cloth, and keep the bird warm and quiet for a few hours. Then remove the cloth gently—do not whisk it off suddenly—and let the bird accustom itself to its new surroundings. Do not crowd up close to the cage at first, or make rapid movements; and do not let several people press up close to the cage to examine the new pet. And keep quiet.

It is important to find out from the dealer, or from the former owner, what bird's diet was; keep it on the same diet for a few days, gradually changing over to the standard foods recommended for the species. If the bird seems to be in a rather run-down condition—that is, if it sits on its perch more or less fluffed up, or merely sits listlessly, and seems to lack alertness—then it should be fed for a few days on some soft and easily digested food, say boiled rice, or oats, or corn. At the same time a mild stimulant might be given for a day or two, about twelve or fifteen drops of brandy in the drinking water (a drinking cupful), or any mild tonic which is recommended. At such times, keep the bird carefully away from cool drafts, and at all times out of rooms filled with tobacco smoke, heavy frying odors, fumes from oil or gas stoves, and dust. Remove the bird from a room which you are dusting or sweeping. Also keep the bird away from very bright lights, hot stuffy places, or places where there is a good deal of noise and bustle.

Choosing a Parrot

Space will not permit here a detailed description of the various kinds of desirable parrots, but we will mention the kinds which for one reason or another, have proved the most popular with bird lovers. Some persons want a talking parrot, while others want only a bright colored and cozy little pet bird, and do not care whether it talks or not.

I. The Best Talkers

These are listed in the order of their ability and teachableness, but it must be remembered that opinions may differ slightly.

1. African Gray Parrot. Probably the best all-around parrot as far as vocal ability is concerned. It is conceded by nearly all to be the one which learns to sing and whistle best; though its talking abilities, while superb, are thought by others not to be of the very first quality.

2. Levaillant's Amazon Parrot.

3. Mexican Double Yellow-Head. This bird is said to possess a voice more nearly like the human voice —though this is a matter of opinion. However, the Yellow-Head is a superb talker, and by some is placed at the very head of the class. Another feature is that

35

it has a very gentle disposition; this cannot be said of all parrots.

4. Cuban Amazon Parrot.

5. Panama Parrot. These lovely green parrots are very teachable, and are valued by some more highly than any other parrot, for they combine extreme striking plumage with excellent talking ability. They are not quite such good singers and whistlers as the African Gray Parrot or the Mexican Double Yellow-Head.

6. Cuban Amazon, or Cuban Parrot. A strikingly colored bird; bright green with a red throat and white forehead. Only a second-rate talker, but a good whistler and singer and imitator of all kinds of sounds.

II. The Gentle and Quieter Parrots

These make the best pets; they are affectionate and easily tameable.

1. Lovebirds. These are not the Shell Parakeets, or Budgerigars (though these birds are often called Lovebirds also), but are a sort of dwarf, chunky parrot; with large head and short tail. They look rather funny and top-heavy. These birds get along very amiably when there are several in a single cage, and are kept because they make such quiet domestic-acting little pets.

2. Shell Parakeets, or Budgerigars, or Budgies, sometimes also called Lovebirds, or merely Parakeets. There are some two hundred or more of these delicate graceful little parrot-like birds, with fat faces, short recurved bills and long slender tails; to say nothing of the delicate, striking colors. It would be useless to list more than a few of the more popular kinds here, for the choice is wide, and people's tastes in colors vary.

3. Blue Parakeets:

Cobalt Blue. Rather deep all-over color, with upper parts lighter.

Azure Blue. Upper parts whitish, under parts delicate pale blue.

4. Green Parakeets: The most popular of these is the Grass Green Parakeet, a lovely bright green bird, with its upper parts yellow.

5. Yellow Parakeets. The Canary Yellow Parakeet is by far the most popular member of the yellow group. The entire body of this bird is a bright canary yellow; but the tips of the wings are pure white; the tail is also white. There are green and red patches about the face.

6. White Parakeets. The White Shell Parakeet is the best of these. The entire body is white, with little bluish patches about the side of the head.

7. Mauve Parakeets. The Mauve Shell Parakeets are perhaps not as popular as the lighter, brighter colors; yet many people own them, to complete a color collection or for breeding. The upper parts are whitish, the lower parts mauve.

The above parakeets are the ones usually seen in dealers' establishments; but there are many others which one can buy, if one has the means to do so. The best way to determine what kinds of parakeets you wish to own is to consult a color chart of these birds. An excellent chart of this kind showing nineteen of the most likeable kinds of parakeets is published at Bird Haven, Reseda, California. See Bibliography, page 111.

HOUSING

THERE are numerous ways in which Parrot-like birds can be housed and kept successfully ; each method will be dealt with separately in the following paragraphs. Individual birds and species can be spoiled if not suitably housed to the needs of their kind. A great deal of the success with talking pets depends on the correct and most comfortable accommodation. It should always be remembered that birds which are not comfortable and happy will never make good talkers.

CAGES

For pet Parrots of the African Grey and Amazon kinds, the conventional round or square all-wire cages are by far the most suitable type to use. The actual size of the cages varies according to the size of the bird which is to be housed. As a general rule the size for the big Amazon Parrots and the big Cockatoos should not be less than 20 ins. square at the base and 30 ins. to 36 ins. in height. For the Greys and ordinary-sized Amazons, etc., the base should not be less than 18 ins. square and 26 ins. to 30 ins. in height. For Ring-necks, Senegals, etc., the base should be not less than 16 ins. to 18 ins. square and the height 24 ins. to 26 ins. Lovebirds, Budgerigars and some of the smaller kinds of Parrakeets do very well in the large-sized all-wire canary cages. Lories and Lorikeets need a special type of cage because of the nature of their droppings. These cages are of the box type fitted with a sand draw on which absorbent paper is fixed. It will be realised that the cages for the large Parrots, Cockatoos and Parrakeets must be constructed of very heavy gauge wire because of the birds' powerful beaks. Fig. 12 gives the general layout of an all-wire square parrot cage. It is usual to have a large-mesh wire grill just above the removable sand tray to prevent escape when being cleaned and at the same time to allow the droppings to fall unhindered on to the sand tray. The perches are made of hardwood, preferably oak, and have metal caps at each end to prevent the birds from gnawing them away. The round wire cages are made on the same principle as the square, the only difference being their shape. It is essential that the doors of cages are fitted with a clip for fastening that is guarded by a shield, so that the birds cannot open the cage from the inside. If this is not done it is surprising how quickly the birds will discover how to open the door and allow themselves liberty at the most inopportune times. Parrot cages are all fitted at the top

Fig. 12.

ALL-WIRE CAGE

with a ring for hanging, but generally speaking the birds prefer to have their cages standing solidly on a firm table. The reason for this would seem to be that the birds prefer to be nearer to their owners and also they are likely to get more attention at table level. Although Lovebirds, Budgerigars and small Parrakeets thrive very well in large, all-wire canary cages, quite a lot of people prefer to house their birds in oblong wood and wire box cages. These cages are usually 24 ins. long, 15 ins. high, 12 ins. deep, with the top, bottom, back and sides of wood and the front made of a removable wire panel, see Fig. 13. All wood used for cage making should be good, well-seasoned hardwood, for it is surprising how even small birds will find a soft spot and gnaw their way to liberty. Although these box-type cages may not be so decorative as the all-wire ones they have the advantage of preventing all draughts from reaching the birds.

STANDS

Large birds like Macaws, large Cockatoos and Parrots are mostly trained to live on big " T "-shaped stands complete with sand trays, see Fig. 14. These stands consist of an upright of tubular steel set in a heavy base and fixed to a round metal sand tray of the same diameter as the

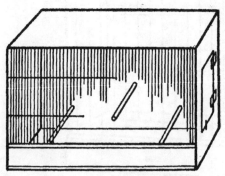

Fig. 13. BOX TYPE CAGE

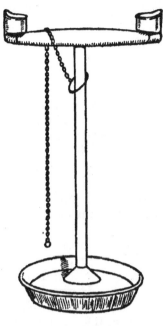

Fig. 14. STAND

" T " of the perch. This perch is usually made of well-seasoned oak, or similar hardwood, and at each end are fixed metal seed and water containers with removable porcelain linings. The birds are kept under control by a light steel chain which is clipped to the bird's leg at one end with a swivel clip, and the other is allowed to run free on a large ring which is fixed round the metal upright of the stand. These stands do certainly give the Macaws and the larger Parrots plenty of room for full wing exercise which would not be possible in an ordinary-sized wire parrot cage. As a change from their usual perch, birds often use the metal upright as a climbing post and this they can do quite easily as the chain ring will slide up and down. The use of stands is the most convenient way of keeping large Parrot-like birds indoors. It must be stated here, provided the birds are trained to a stand, being chained by one leg in no way inconveniences them and they are perfectly happy and live to a great age in perfect condition with this kind of accommodation.

AVIARIES

Specially constructed aviaries whether indoor or outdoor are needed to house most of the large Parrots, Macaws, Cockatoos and larger Parrakeets because of the power of their beaks. Birds of the calibre of Macaws can cut through ordinary wire netting like a knife through butter and need heavy gauge metal bars to enclose them with safety. Any woodwork used in the construction of these aviaries must be hard, strong and well seasoned and protected on the outside by metal sheeting. The best material for building the sleeping or shelter quarters is brick, as it is practically indestructible by the birds and the cost is quite reasonable. Small Parrots, Parrakeets, Lovebirds, etc., can be housed in Budgerigar-type aviaries if strongly built and wired with good quality wire netting, see Fig. 15. It may be necessary to double wire certain places in these aviaries and also to wire any woodwork that comes within the reach of the beaks of the birds. The majority of perches should be made of hard wood so that they need not be renewed continuously.

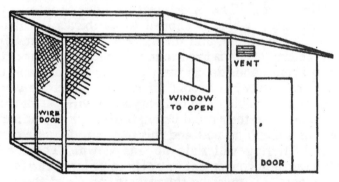

Fig. 15. STANDARD AVIARY

However, it is a good thing to have a few soft wood perches for the birds to gnaw and amuse themselves.

Aviaries are mostly used for the breeding of Parrot-like birds, and it is really surprising how many different kinds have already reared young successfully in captivity. Quite a number of species have also bred in large indoor pens ; by this method many more breeding pairs can be housed in a given space. Water vessels used in pens and aviaries should be large and shallow to facilitate bathing which gives all Parrot-like birds great enjoyment. Some breeders give their birds small water vessels near their seed vessels and an entirely separate one for bathing in another part of their enclosure. This arrangement is a good one as it ensures the birds always having clean drinking water. The floor covering of aviaries varies according to their size ; large ones having grassed flights and sanded concrete sleeping quarters and smaller ones all sanded concrete. Care must be taken to ensure that breeding and sleeping quarters are free from vermin. Although mice will not attack large birds they will very often disturb them whilst nesting, causing them to leave their eggs or even their young. A concreted floor together with small ($\frac{1}{2}$-in.) mesh wire netting 18 ins. up the sides of all the wooden structures, will make them safe against the larger vermin. Any mice which invade the enclosures can be exterminated by the careful placing of *covered* traps. The inside brick or woodwork of aviaries should be decorated with limewash or good quality distemper. However, if paint is used it should be of a nonpoisonous kind as many lead-base paints can be harmful to birds if eaten. Wire and metal work from which all loose pieces of galvanising have been brushed can be preserved by painting with one of the many good bituminous paints now obtainable from all high-class paint stores.

Training

As soon as parakeets were isolated from their parakeet friends and found themselves with no one to coo at and converse with in parakeet-talk, they took naturally to mimicking the sounds made by their owners. This ability to mimic and imitate sounds is inherent in the parakeet species. Time and patience is all that is required to develop your bird's ability to talk. Don't expect miracles overnight or you will be disappointed. But if you combine patience, time and kindness, the results you get will truly seem a miracle.

BE CONSISTENT

Your parakeet is an individual with a unique personality all his own. Keep this in mind at all times. You will soon discover how quick his responses are and to which methods he responds most rapidly and agreeably. Be consistent in your method of training him. If you are firm one day and coaxing the next, the result will be a confused bird, and an untrained one. Strike a balance in your approach, follow through with it, and you will find there are almost endless training possibilities open to you and your pet. A little effort on your part

in the beginning will be repaid in the pleasure and pride your budgie will afford you for years to come.

Before going on with some basic rules on training your parakeet, there are a few mistaken notions about parakeets that should be clarified:

MALE AND FEMALE WILL TALK

It is not true that only the male will talk. This is a superstition that started because only the male canary is the singer. However, the female parakeet will talk as well as the male, and sometimes better. You hear more about the male as a talker because many owners taught only the males. Sex makes no difference in the ability of a parakeet to talk.

It is not true that it is necessary to get a parakeet just out of the nest to be able to tame it and teach it to talk. You can do as well with a bird several months old. If you do start with a parakeet who is a few months old, rather than a few weeks old, you have the added assurance that he has been completely weaned past the baby stage and will be that much surer of survival.

A parakeet is not "old" if the lines, or ridges, across the forehead have disappeared and the solid crown has taken its place. This happens from three to four months after birth so that a parakeet five months old will appear much the same as a bird several years old.

Color makes no difference in a parakeet's ability to talk or be trained. All budgies have the same aptitude, no matter what their coloration.

TAMING COMES FIRST

Let us return now to some things you should know about training your bird. The first step is taming the budgie. Rarely will a budgie talk until you have won his confidence and affection—until he is tame and enjoys your company.

It is best to give your budgie about two weeks time to settle down and get used to his new cage, after first bringing him into your home. During this period do little more than care for his needs and show him your affection, making him feel at home and becoming friendly with him.

Remember, at all times be gentle; do not make sudden movements and, above all, talk to him in a kindly, soft spoken manner. At first, take a wood stick or perch and while talking softly, work the stick into his cage. He will soon become accustomed to this and will light on it. The next step is the most important because, once successful, you are well on your way towards having a tame and talking parakeet. This is to coax the budgie on the finger when you put your hand in the cage.

Reach your finger into the cage slowly and gradually, until he is no longer frightened at its presence. You may stroke his head or breast and in a very short time he is ready to perch on your finger. When he does, show him your approval by rewarding him with a treat food or delicacy he particularly likes.

STRETCHING HIS WINGS

He is now ready to leave his cage. Fasten back the cage door and let him perch on your finger. Slowly—work your hand, with the bird on it, out of the cage.

The first few times he flies around the room, he will probably fly wildly, until exhausted. He will either fall to the floor or perch on some high object. If he falls to the floor, talk to him reassuringly as you gently retrieve him. If he lights on some high object, softly push him off with the training stick and he will either fly back to your hand or return to his cage. If you secure a landing strip on the outside of the cage, your budgie will soon learn to land there.

Do not rush the training period. Be patient and kindly toward him always as you must keep the affection and confidence of your bird. Remember these lovable pets can *sense* kindness and will not permit themselves to be trained unless they are convinced of your love for them.

TEACHING TRICKS

Once your pet has become finger tame, and has learned to fly to your finger after leaving the cage, it is easy to teach him many different stunts and tricks. He will readily climb ladders, walk tightropes, ring bells, ride toy cars and trains, and crawl through a tunnel. All of these training props are inexpensive and will afford you and your parakeet many hours of amusement. Budgies have a natural instinct to push and pull objects—provide him with little cars and wagons he can push to his and your heart's delight.

The number of tricks you can teach a parakeet all depends on you. If you take the time to show him what you expect and supply him with the gadgets, you'll find that before long your budgie has developed a whole circus act. At first you'll have to guide him and show him what to do. It's easy; place the object you want him to carry in his beak, set him on the toy cars you want him to ride, and prod his tail gently to point him in the right direction. Keep repeating the movements until he has learned the trick. Once he has learned a trick he'll be ready to perform at a moment's notice without any help, and he'll probably practice his repertoire when he's alone.

There are three kinds of tricks your parakeet will learn: riding tricks, climbing tricks and beak tricks. All the more complicated and advanced tricks he will later learn with experience and practice are just combinations of these three tricks.

RIDING

This is an easy trick. Start by perching him either on your finger or on his training stick, and slowly bring him to the toy you want him to ride and set him on it. Repeat this for a few minutes. He will soon hop on the vehicle by himself.

CLIMBING

Parakeets are born climbers. They take to climbing up and down the cage rungs immediately. With just a little effort you can adapt this skill into an art. Place your budgie on the bottom rung of a toy ladder, set at an angle. If he holds fast and doesn't move upward, nudge his tail gently with your finger. He'll walk a step or two, and stop. Nudge him again until he climbs to the top non-stop. Teaching him to climb down the ladder will take a little more practice. Place him on the top rung. Chances are he will just perch there. Encircle him gently with your hand and slip your finger under his tail, pushing just a little. Continue this on each step until he makes it down on his own power.

BEAK TRICKS

By providing the proper toys you will soon be able to teach your budgie to push, pull and carry. Hold the bird gently in your hands and press the object you want him to take against his beak until he opens his beak and grasps it. Show him exactly what you want him to do with the toy, and at first, actually make him do it. You'll be surprised at how quickly he catches on.

WING CLIPPING

Some bird fanciers believe it best to clip or pluck the wings of a parakeet before taming. I believe it detracts greatly from their beauty and also injures their feelings. Parakeets were meant to fly. Even if you have acquired an older bird it is possible to train him without wing clipping. And since it requires so little work, it's best to train a parakeet without resorting to wing clipping.

TEACHING YOUR BUDGIE TO TALK

To start your bird on the way to a good vocabulary, pick out one word—just one word that you wish to start with. Use something simple, like "hello" or "baby"—and do not go any further until this word is mastered. Place your pet on your finger and speak very clearly, a little louder than your normal conversational voice, repeat this one word several times. Then, bring your budgie closer to your mouth—let him see your lips as you pronounce this word, and say it over

and over again. After about 15 minutes, place your pet back in his cage.

Naturally, the more time spent in teaching your bird, the sooner he will learn to talk for himself; but don't tire him with overly long sessions. It is best to work with him several times a day—always the same word—repeated clearly and distinctly. Before covering the bird for the night, repeat the word again while he's in his cage.

After he has learned this one word, immediately start him on another word or short phrase. Once the first word is learned, you will find he will learn a complete phrase much more quickly. But always go back to the first word. And continue to go back reviewing and repeating the words he has already learned as he goes on to new words and phrases. The necessity for repetition cannot be overemphasized. It's a good idea to start off a lesson for a new word with a quick review of all the words and phrases he already knows. And after coaching him on the new word, if he doesn't grasp it quickly, just run through the words he is familiar with, and he may surprise you by adding the new word to the list.

AGE MAKES NO DIFFERENCE

There are no set rules on the correct age at which to start

teaching your budgie to talk. A bird of any age can be taught how to talk. But it's usually easier with a younger bird. The best results are obtained from birds under six months. There are, however, many cases of birds whose training started as young as six weeks and as old as three years; and they turned into equally accomplished talkers.

The length of time it takes for a parakeet to learn how to talk will vary. A rare "genius" may learn to say his first word after a week or two, and there are some at the other end who may take from nine months to nearly a year before uttering that first word. The average is about twelve to sixteen weeks for the first word. Don't despair if your budgie doesn't start chatting as quickly as you'd like him to. Budgies are very like humans, and often we find that the slow starters run away with all the prizes.

The first word is the hardest. But no matter how long it takes for your pet to learn that first word, you can be assured that the other words will come easily, and quickly. Once he's caught on to the idea of talking, you'll be able to teach him a new word or phrase every few days. The extent of your parakeet's vocabulary will depend in large part on how much time you are able to spend working with him.

PARAKEET TRAINING RECORD

You can make great strides with your parakeet's education and save yourself time by using the Hartz Mountain "Your Parakeet Can Teach Itself to Talk" training record. The method employed by this record is much the same as the one you would use in teaching your bird to talk—constant repetition in a clear well-spoken voice of a simple word or phrase. When you play the record for your bird for the first time, be sure you are near him to comfort him if he is puzzled at hearing a voice from a source he cannot detect. He will soon grow accustomed to it, and before you know it he will be talking back to the recording machine. If you have a repeat mechanism on your record player, you can play the record over and over again for your bird, even when you are away from home. It will save you many hours of time.

Care and Feeding

You will be surprised at how little time and effort you have to spend in caring for your parakeet. They are hardy creatures and remarkably self-sufficient.

HIS CAGE IS HIS CASTLE

Most any type of cage will do provided it is large enough and well equipped. Place a swing and a ladder in the cage as budgies love to swing and climb. Be sure there are several perches in the cage; they are excellent for strengthening his feet. The cage doors should be hinged in such a manner that they can be left open, permitting your pet to return when he wishes.

The cage should be placed in a light spot, out of the sun. It must be out of a draft. The cage should be placed high, preferably on a cage stand or wall bracket. It is generally believed that budgies like to be covered at night because it affords them privacy and a sense of security.

Every well equipped parakeet cage should contain a seed cup, a treat cup and a water cup. The cups should be kept full at all times, as parakeets are constant nibblers.

CLEANLINESS IS A MUST

Cleanliness is the keynote of parakeet care. Wash and dry the feed and water cups daily. Cleanse the cage periodically. Keeping a good quality gravel paper at the bottom of the cage is an aid to sanitation. Perches have to be kept clean at all times— either scrape them or use a sanded tube refill. The sanded tube refill is highly recommended as the abrasive surface helps trim the bird's claws.

BATHING BUDGIE

Equally important is keeping the budgie clean. Many para-

keet owners are concerned because their pets will not bathe themselves, as canaries do. Many parakeets take naturally to using a bird bath that can be attached to the cage door. If yours won't, I suggest that you use one of the prepared bird spray baths. Make sure that the spray is exceedingly fine and does not gush out, getting into his eyes and frightening him. A bath with a fine misty spray, such as the Hartz Mountain spray bath, is a luxury your pet will enjoy.

A WELL BALANCED DIET

The parakeet of today is a thoroughly domesticated pet. As such, nothing is more important to his well-being than fresh, nourishing seeds, properly cleaned and dust free. By fresh, we do not mean freshly taken from a sack of seed stored for months. It is far better to purchase smaller amounts of commercially packaged seeds, especially mixed for parakeets, and of assured cleanliness. Such mixtures as the nationally advertised Hartz Mountain Parakeet Seed will, in the long run, prove more economical by keeping your bird free of ailments that result from improper food mixtures.

The ideal daily food contains a mixture of canary and millet seeds. Always keep your budgie's seed cup filled. These birds are apt to permit chaff, or hulled seeds, to remain on the top of the seed cup. Make sure that what appears to be a full seed cup is not merely a pile of shelled seeds.

Until your parakeet has gotten used to his cage and learned to find his feed cup, keep an ample supply of seed *on the bottom of the cage.* Many young birds have been known to starve in the midst of plenty by not being able to locate the feed cup.

Parakeets require additional food and seed elements. Wild grass seeds, oats or oat groats and wild foreign seed delicacies should be fed in smaller quantities to your pet. This stimulates his appetite and provides the balanced diet essential for his well-being. The Hartz Mountain Parakeet Treat contains such a mixture and is highly recommended by many aviarists who keep a small treat cup of this food before their birds at all times.

Parakeets require a good grade of gravel of correct texture and size. Since parakeets have no teeth, the gravel enters the bird's gizzard and grinds his food. Keep an ample supply on the bottom of the cage rather than in a container. Budgies like the feel of gravel underfoot and it is well for them to scratch around and walk on.

Successful breeders insist on a millet spray hung from the cage. This is the nearest we can come to providing your pet with the same food, in the same form, he would find in his wild state. He will relish picking the seed from the stalks. Cod liver oil, also a necessity in your bird's diet, is found in Hartz Mountain Condition Food.

Another essential is a cuttlebone. Cuttlebone is the shell of the cuttlefish, found in the Mediterranean Sea. A piece of cuttlebone should hang in the cage at all times. It is a source of calcium and other salts which will benefit your bird. It will keep his beak strong and hard and his bones strong. An additional source of minerals and salts is the Mineral Keet Kake, which can be attached to the cage within easy reach of the bird.

Greens are advisable, but they should be fed sparingly and

always be sure they are washed and dried before feeding; some greens are often sprayed with harmful chemicals. The tops of any green vegetables except lettuce and parsley are recommended. Lettuce and parsley may sometimes cause diarrhea. At the first sign of looseness in a bird's droppings, discontinue all greens at once and mix a good amount of uncooked oatmeal in his seed until diarrhea has disappeared.

A fresh supply of water should be available at all times in the water cup of his cage. The water cup must be cleaned and rinsed daily.

Ailments AND HOW TO TREAT THEM

Parakeets are very hardy birds. They are seldom stricken by illness or ailments. If your budgie is properly cared for he will live a long and healthy life, from 15 to 25 years, and a healthy one. Some occasional illnesses may develop because of the owner's carelessness with his little charge. The parakeet's resistance to disease always goes hand in hand with a good state of nutrition. For this reason, it is so important for you to follow the rules for your bird's diet which we have gone into thoroughly in the preceding chapter "Care and Feeding".

Here is a brief outline of some of the most common parakeet ailments, their symptoms, and how to treat them. Should your parakeet become ill, with proper treatment, recovery will be rapid.

COLDS

Colds are generally caused by exposing the parakeet to a draft. Budgies can withstand low temperatures, but never a draft.

Symptoms: Looks puffed up—listless—partly closed eyes—ruffled feathers; if the cold is severe, one or both eyes may blacken. As soon as the cold is cured, this blackness will disappear.

Ailments AND HOW TO TREAT THEM

Treatment: The bird must be kept warm, in even temperature day and night. Provide fresh, tepid water daily. Feed Hartz Mountain KEET-LIFE, Medicated Seed alternating with Hartz Mountain Diet, as directed on label of KEET-LIFE. Keep in cage until the cold clears.

CONSTIPATION

Symptoms: Infrequent and hard droppings, general listlessness.
Treatment: Add more greens to the diet. If constipation is severe, give him one or two drops of mineral oil with a medicine dropper. Allow him more exercise.

DEFECTIVE BEAKS

You will observe the beak is overgrown or misshapen. This will not harm your pet, but will detract from his appearance. You can trim his beak with a sharp manicuring scissors or a nail clipper; this does not hurt the bird.

DIARRHEA

Symptoms: Loose droppings, soiled vent feathers; he will be inactive and sit with his feathers ruffled up, his eyes partly closed.
Treatment: Remove all green foods immediately. Keep the bird warm. Provide Hartz Mountain KEET-LIFE, Medicated Seed along with Hartz Mountain Diet, as directed on label of KEET-LIFE. Some aviarists advise boiled water or boiled milk until completely cured.

EYE SORES

Eye sores are very rare in parakeets. They may result from an eyelash being turned under, or in some instances from insect bites.

Ailments AND HOW TO TREAT THEM

Treatment: Clean the area twice daily with sterile cotton or gauze that has been saturated or dipped in mercurochrome.

FRENCH MOULT

There is much disagreement about the cause of this disease: some experts say it is caused by improper diet, and others argue it is caused by a mite.

Symptoms: French Moult attacks only very young birds and causes them to lose their wing feathers, before or immediately after they leave the nest. These budgies' growth is stunted, and because they do not have their primary wing feathers they are unable to fly.

No treatment for this disease has yet been discovered. If you buy a budgie who is fully feathered and able to fly, you need have no worries about his suffering from French Moult.

MITES

Parakeets, unlike other caged birds, are seldom bothered by these parasites. Many times they are suspected because parakeets preen and pick themselves. A hand lens may be used to distinguish between lice, which have three pair of legs, and mites, which have four pair, in the adult stage.

Treatment: If mites are present, remove the bird from his cage and clean him thoroughly, preferably with a prepared solution such as the Hartz Mountain My-T-Mite Powder. Clean the cage with boiling water and disinfect with a good disinfectant. Be sure the cage is thoroughly dry before returning the bird. Replace all perches and toys with new ones.

PNEUMONIA

Pneumonia is an illness caused by a specific agent.

Symptoms: The same as for a cold, but when the lungs are infected, the budgie will gasp for breath and wheeze.

Ailments AND HOW TO TREAT THEM

Treatment: Keep bird quiet and warm, at an even temperature of from 80° to 85°. Provide Hartz Mountain KEET-LIFE, Medicated Seed along with Hartz Mountain Diet, as directed on label of KEET-LIFE. Add Hartz Mountain Bird Tonic to his drinking water.

CUTTING TOENAILS:

If your bird's nails become too long use a scissor to cut them to the proper length. Hold the bird against the light so you can see the vein. Cut the part of the nail that is right near the vein.

Household Safety Hints

Let us dwell for a while on a few precautions you can take to avoid the heartbreak that would come if your pet met with an accident in your home.

It should be a rule never to leave your budgie out of his cage when you are away from home. The tiny creature is apt to get into serious trouble if he is unguarded. Budgies will perch on door tops; this can be disastrous if the wind blows the door shut, or someone slams the door.

It is best not to allow your parakeet to fly around a room with a large mirror in it. The bird may fly directly into it, with serious consequences.

Always be sure that all outside doors and unscreened windows are closed before allowing your parakeet out of his cage. Should your bird get outside, he would fly high and the chances are that he would not find his way back home.

Running water from a faucet will attract budgies. They love flying through it. Guard against their getting this habit as they may get scalded if the water is hot.

Make it a point not to allow your parakeet the freedom of

Household Safety Hints

the kitchen when you are working there. Many of the common household appliances that you use every day can spell injury or death. Such electrical appliances as mixers, irons, fans and vacuum cleaners are particularly dangerous.

Budgies will, as a rule, ignore potted plants. But if there are insufficient greens in his diet, he may munch on your prize philodendron. It is best for both the plant and the budgie not to keep them in the same room.

Breeding

More and more people every day are joining the growing cult of parakeet breeders. Whether you start with one pair in a single breeding cage, or a few dozen pairs in large breeding aviaries, you will be amazed at the fun and surprised at the profits this fascinating hobby will bring you.

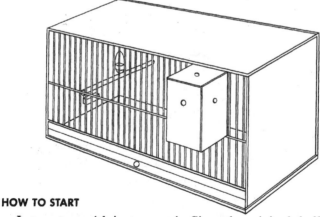

HOW TO START

Let us start with just one pair. Since the original shell parakeet was green, we suggest you start with a pair of this color.

The breeding of no other caged bird requires so little time or money. The initial investment, including the cost of breeding stock, is nominal. And the upkeep will run to *less than 2¢ a day*. Your initial pair of birds need not be expensive show winners. Purchase from a reputable store a pair of strong, healthy birds of unrelated stock. You can go into the fancier points of parakeet breeding after you've had experience; but insist on a healthy pair to start.

The cage should be at least 16 x 16 x 25, or as large as you like. Equip it with the necessary seed, water and treat cups, sliding tray at the bottom, perches, and a plate to secure the nest box.

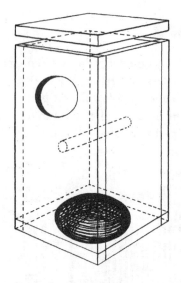

THE NEST BOX

The nest box is a very simple structure—approximately 5 or 6 inches wide, 5 or 6 inches deep and about 8 or 10 inches high. The entrance hole should be cut out about an inch or two from the top, at the front of the box. Directly under this hole, you can attach a two or three inch perch. The bottom of the nest box must be concave; you should hollow out a round or oval shaped base about ½ inch deep and from 4 to 5 inches across. It is advisable to have a removable top on this box. The nest box should be fastened either at the sides or back of the cage.

Contrary to stories you hear about the best time of year to start breeding, provided proper heating is available at all times, it makes no difference if you start in Spring or Mid-Winter. For an outdoor aviary, March or April is the best time to start.

If the pair of parakeets prove compatible, you will notice them visiting the nest box after a few days. Wait a day or two before lifting the top of the nest box. You will probably see some eggs, and you can expect to find an additional egg every other day until about six eggs have been laid.

The incubation period is 18 days, but we suggest you do not remove the eggs for at least 10 days longer.

When the baby birds emerge from their shells they are bare of feathers. It takes almost a week before the first signs of down are seen and almost another week before feathers start to appear.

THE PARENTS DO ALL THE WORK

No special food is required for the baby birds, as the mother budgie feeds her young herself by regurgitating food. About a week after the last egg has been hatched, the mother bird leaves the nest quite frequently and the father bird takes over the feeding of the young. Parental feeding continues for 4 or 5 weeks, and then the babies are able to feed themselves. Quite often the mother bird will begin to lay a second batch of eggs before her young have left the nest. If this happens, you should remove the young from the nest and clean the nest box thoroughly to make it ready for the next clutch of eggs.

A mother bird will occasionally become egg-bound. Heat and mineral oil are the prescribed treatment. Place a drop or two of mineral oil directly into the bird's beak and a like amount in its vent. Put the mother bird in a small cage, with all the perches removed, so that she will stay at the bottom of the cage. A soft cloth should cover the bottom of the cage and the cage should be set over a hot water bottle or electric heater.

The condition will soon be relieved and you will see the egg come from the mother.

We suggest that you permit your parakeets to raise no more than 2 or 3 nests of birds each year. This insures strong, healthy stock, and will not be too trying on the parent birds.

BREEDING ON A LARGER SCALE

Should you want to enlarge the scope of your breeding activities, change from the single breeding cage to the large aviary, or bird house, and add as many pairs of parakeets as you like. The care of the parents and baby birds will remain the same. You should provide a house about 6 or 7 feet wide, 6 feet high and 10 to 14 feet long. Hang your nest boxes along one wall. Make sure to add an extra male bird to your colony, as nothing can more disrupt an aviary than one jealous or unmated female.

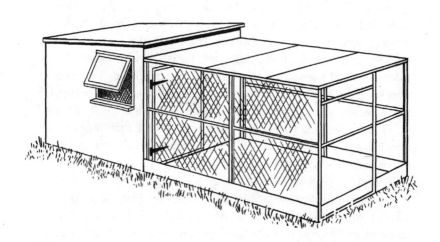

COLOR BREEDING

If you plan to breed parakeets, or budgies, on a small scale, you won't get much chance to experiment for color. For purposes of general information, however, or if you should breed on a larger scale, the following data will prove of interest.

From the dark green of the original Australian parakeet, mutations have developed a large variety of other colors or strains, which are today standards themselves.

Green, as you know, comes from the blending of blue and yellow. These colors have been isolated in the selected breeding of parakeets, and by crossing and recrossing these three basic colors, green, blue and yellow, many new strains were developed. The parakeets you see today in such varied colors as mint green, chartreuse, olive green, turquoise, sky blue, mauve, pale yellow, dark yellow and violet, are all descended, by careful color breeding, from the original Australian shell parakeet.

Parakeets of different colors will inter-breed freely. This has helped make color progress relatively simple. But the green color always remains the prevailing influence in all matings. When a true green is mated to a yellow or a blue, the babies will all be green, but their offspring will be able to produce birds the color of their other parent.

The offspring of these pure green and blue matings are called Splits, and are designated as green/blue, signifying that green is the color of the bird and blue denotes its ability to produce blue birds when suitably mated.

The darker color is always dominant in parakeet breeding. There is always the possibility of a pair of parakeets throwing a Sport which, when mated with other birds, might throw an entirely new color. Aviarists are trying for blacks, reds and pinks. But with the exception of an odd Sport, these colors have not yet been developed as a definite strain.

Color breeding is a vast field for the budding aviarist. Nothing can equal the thrill your adventures in color breeding will bring you. The variety of colors you can develop in your own aviary will be a never-ending source of pleasure. And there is always the possibility that you may come up with an entirely new color strain.